THE SORROWS OF SLAVERY

"Poetry of the Past"

Benjamin Franklin Burum, JR

The Historic Black Poet

Greatness University Publishers

London, UK

www.greatnessuniversity.co.uk

ISBN: 978-1-913164-40-9

ISBN-13: 978-1-913164-40-9

DEDICATION

I dedicate this book to the more than 100 Million Slaves that lost their lives due to the *Transatlantic Slave Trade*, as well as the other slave trades that took place before this time, such as the, *Sub-Sahara Slave Trade and Native American Slave Trade.* In this day and time, as some publishers attempts to bury the wrongs of slavery by calling Slaves; "workers", the truth must still be told. Instead of sweeping truth under the rug, I choose to keep truth alive, by expressing my perspective of the Sorrows of Slavery.

CONTENTS

Acknowledgments i

Decreasing Cargo 3

Master Made me Free 5

Watery Grave Freed Slave 7

Backman so Strong 9

Freedom I Crave 11

When you want to be Free 13

Constantly Pray 15

New Lynch Mentality 17

The Land of the Free 21

Slave Trade 23

Free Again 26

One Day at a Time 28

He Calls us Savage Beast 31

Master's Child Favors Me 33

Hey Master 35

They Say 37

The Last Laugh of 1963 41

Free Labor Slave 44

It Won't be Long 47

In Due Time 49

Blessing for Me 51

The Sorrows of Slavery

African Drum	53
The Very First Snow	55
Freedom Bound	57
To Get my Freedom	59
The Son he Never Set Free	61
10-Lashes of Pain	63
The Building of this Country	66
I May Be Satisfied	69
The True 4th of July	73
Last and Evil Days	75
Freedom Cheers	78
Early in the Morning	81
White Friends and Family	83
Broken Down Reservation	85
If I was Free	87
Your Last Breath	89
Before Sunrise	92
Freedom I Truly Adore	94
Harriet Tubman	96
Black Kings and Queens	100
Black Woman	103
Strong Woman	106

ACKNOWLEDGMENTS

First and foremost, I would like to give all the Glory to the Most-High God of Abraham, Isaac and Jacob for giving me the ability and strength to complete this task. Secondly, I would like to acknowledge my wife and Kids, who has pushed me to get this work of art into a book format that I thought was only a hobby. Thirdly, I would like to acknowledge my other family members, friends and co-workers that listened to me recite some of my work during Black History Month. And last, I would also like to acknowledge Greatness University for allowing me to express my greatness in book form.

DECREASING CARGO

If you saw the movie Amistad, there was a scene that showed a group of slaves brought on deck chained together. As they stood there in awe a slippery substance was thrown on the deck making it difficult for them to stand. Then the ships anchor that was attached to the end of the slave chain, was tossed into the ocean, as all those slaves slipped into their water grave. This poem describes how the lives of 50 purposely drowned slaves was looked at by the white-man as unneeded cargo.

DECREASING CARGO

Today they brought 50-of us above deck,
And just when my eyes began to focus, as I began to look around,
A slippery substance is placed beneath our feet causing all 50 of us to fall-down.
"Decrease the cargo by 50!" is what someone had said,
As we slide into the water, chained together, I knew that all 50 of us would be dead,
Resting on the ocean floor, as we all fight and struggle,
Knowing that we will be free in a different way, with the decrease in oxygen bubbles,
Is this right? The thing I need to know!
When 50 slaves lose their lives, the Whiteman calls it DECREASING CARGO.

MASTER MADE ME FREE

When slaves were taken away from Africa in chains, many had a belief in a High Power (GOD) that created all men free. So, to submit totally and call someone else MASTER was out of the question for most Africans. This poem explains the mentality of a strong slave who understands, regardless of how far that slave ship takes him, he will keep his independent belief of GOD being the True Master of His Life.

MASTER MADE ME FREE

This boat that I did not ask to get on
Has taken me out to sea, so far and beyond
Beyond to a point, with these chains I'm dragging,
Beyond to a point that I can't even imagine,
I can't even think straight, because these chains,
Cause me pain.
He said, "Call him Master!"
But he ain't, and never will be,
Because, THE MASTER I SERVE MADE ALL MEN FREE!

WATERY GRAVE-FREED SLAVE

The slave in this poem speaks on the behalf of the countless number of slaves that lost their lives during storms. When the ship went down, slaves were still chained and could not make escape. Although they perished, death was a form of freedom in their watery grave.

WATERY GRAVE-FREED SLAVE

As this ship begins to sink slowly, I have no means of survival
Because, I'm chained to the hull of this ship; as the water rises higher and higher.
Now I'm off to a watery grave with freedom on my mind,
Even if I could break these chains, there wouldn't be enough time.
For me to get away,
So, I stay, and pray,
And as my tears mix with the salty waters of better days,
I inhale to take my last breath before I pass-away,
Those chains were finally broken when that ship went down,
Giving me freedom for eternity, as I proceed to drown
In my watery grave...
Now I am a FREED-SLAVE.

BLACKMAN SO STRONG

The slave in this poem has heard the Whiteman refer to America as; "The Land of the Free," but could not understand it. Because he is in chains on an auction block ready to be sold like an object. He then thinks about the inventions that would be created by slaves, but only their masters would be able to take the credit for it. He goes from sad to mad, but then realizes that it takes a strong-mined person to deal with the level of mistreatment this country has inflected upon Blacks.

BLACKMAN SO STRONG

I never imagine a place called the land of the free,
Where I stand nude on an auction block as they bet money on me
Examining my body like an animal as I stand,
Why can't they realize, I am nothing but a man.
My skin maybe dark and my hair maybe nappy,
But being forced to call another man "Master" makes me very unhappy.
Now as I look out of my window, and also my door,
At all the inventions that I have made and can't even take credit for.
It makes me mad,
And sometimes it even makes me sad,
Because this land that we are in of the so called Free
Has not always allowed Blacks the best of an opportunity,
But still I must move on,
Even though the journey is long,
I must be considered that BLACKMAN SO STRONG.

FREEDOM I CRAVE

After slaved were beaten with leather straps, salt was poured into their wounds to speed up the healing process. The slave in this poem has just been beaten, as he goes through the healing process, he thinks of all the things he has lost because of slavery, but being a Strong Black Man, his desire for freedom will never go away.

FREEDOM I CRAVE

After my back has been cut with cows-hide,
Salt is poured into my wounds, and the tears run from my eyes,
I scream out loud,
Because it helps me ease the pain.
Cry I do, because I must never mention my true name,
Now it is his name,
That I must claim,
And call my own,
While working as a slave, building his country from dust to dawn,
So, this game I must play, until the day I am free,
As I keep hope alive, by holding it inside of me,
But my visions of Africa will never fade away,
Because, freedom I crave every night and every DAY

WHEN YOU WANT TO BE FREE

The slave in this poem finds comfort in the night-time hours, when the moon and stars light up the sky. But when morning comes, the reality of him only being prized-cattle for the white-man is a fact, but he wants to be free.

WHEN YOU WANT TO BE FREE

Whenever the light of the night
Hits my face I pace,
Back and forth, analyzing a trip to freedom in my mind
But as the sun begins to rise
And shine
Upon my face,
I know that I am in a place,
That I do not wish to be in,
Is it because of my beautiful black skin?
Or am I serving due time for my ancestors' sins?
Chains forced upon me,
Annihilations of whole communities,
I have seen with my eyes,
That is why I'm considered to be, the white man's prize.
Truthfully, this is not my dream,
And happiness is not always what it seems to be, especially, when you WANT TO BE FREE....

CONSTANTLY PRAY

The slave in this poem captures the pain that has been inflicted upon Black men and Women in this country during slavery. Regardless of what has happened to them in the bandage of slavery, they still put their faith in GOD, by knowing, if they constantly pray, their freedom will come one day.

CONSTANTLY PRAY

Persecuted by the scums of this land
Trying to survive I am a strong black man,
With these lashes on my back
These bruises on my neck hands and feet,
I have worked against my will, in the hot-
summer's heat.
It is in my nature to run and to be free,
Although I have been robbed of my Jerusalem
Destiney
Raped out of lust,
Yes, you know how,
My strong black-woman must bear a half-
bread-child.
Reminisce I have of better days to come,
Hopping that one day my people will become
one,
Although they say,
I'll be free someday,
But until that time comes, I must
CONSTANTLY PRAY.

NEW LYNCH MENTALITY

A man by the name of Willie Lynch sent out a letter that outlined several points for slave owners to keep their slaves in check. This poem recognizes the fact that in this day and time, regardless of how much Black communities express their ideas of Lynch's ideas, the negative effects are still being felt. But now instead of being victims of old scare tactics, they inflict this New Lynch Mentality on themselves in the form of illegal activities. This new lynch mentality is destroying our communities at an alarming rate. So, we must recognize that some of the blame of our community's downfall is on us.

NEW LYNCH MENTALITY

The true struggle of my people,
Has been due to the fact, that another has not treated us as an equal,
But as an unwanted stain.
A burden upon those who rule,
Like UN-GODLY fools,
And then they tried to use the Bible as a brainwashing tool,
What right do they have to take my freedom?
What right do they have to treat me unequal?
None, what-so-ever.
And to make things better,
They never knew how cleaver, this field-hand could be,
Until voting for blacks became a reality,
And the ones who couldn't deal with the laws anymore, Dressed up in white robes and masks and burned crosses outside black-folks' doors.
But that still didn't stop us from doing what we had to do,

Until they found out what held black families together like glue,
So, then they flooded it with liquid and powered crack,
They gave our children guns, so now they began to carjack,
Now from the young, the old, the mighty and the weak,
It's hard to believe that so many of our people are six feet,
Deep beneath the earth's crust,
But don't cause a fuss, put some of the blame on us,
Because a lot of the problems that we currently see,
Is a direct result of a modern day; WILLIE LYNCH MENTALITY.

THE LAND OF THE FREE

My great grandmother told me a story of how a group of white men befriended an African King and asked for his help in building his county. When the white-man introduced the system called Indentured Servitude, the King saw it as a means of assisting his kingdom by allowing some of his servants to get a piece of the American Dream in the Land of the Free. But the greed of the white-man caused him to terminate the contract and use his power to de-crown and enslave the King too.

THE LAND OF THE FREE

All I can remember is me,
I was a King in my country,
My strong black woman a Queen being all she could be.
Then one day
Another man came my way,
He presented himself as a friend in need,
But not sharing his thoughts of evil dirty deeds,
He explained to me,
This thing,
Called indentured servitude,
Saying, we would work for a while and never be treaded cruel,
Then we were taken upon a boat, so we could sail across the sea,
In chains we were bonded and shipped off to the land of the free,
The home of the brave,
The land of the white appointed master's and DE-CROWNED BLACK SLAVES.

SLAVE TRADE

Although some Kingdoms in Africa played a role in the slave trade. Many of the Slaves were from certain kingdoms. Some African Kings saw their slaves as servants who were treated with respect and given options more like workers. So, when they sold slaves to the Europeans, some never thought of the inhumane this that would happen to them. The slave in this poem sees how his king was double-crossed and forced into slavery.

SLAVE TRADE

Thinking of the days,
Of the slave trade,
Has made my mind wonder:
You see, some of the kings in my country
Did sell me into slavery,
But they never thought of the inhumane things that would happen to me,
Like being caged like an animal and thrown into the sea.
I guess my king should have thought twice
About doing business with a man that seemed so nice,
Because now that I'm in slaved, I see my old king too,
Saying; "You should never sell off your people,
Because it JUST MIGHT HAPPEN TO YOU."

FREE AGAIN

This poem explains how slaves did things to express their dislike for their slave master, by running away or breaking tools on purpose. All acts of rebellion had serious consequences, mainly a set number of lashes. The slave in this poem has been met with the punishment of being whipped regardless of how many lashes he receives; he turns to GOD and pray for the day he can be Free Again.

FREE AGAIN

The true concept of my imagination
Is due to the fact, that, this; particular;
situation,
Has caused a strain
On my brain, and to distance myself from this
tragedy
I can only try and distort the reality,
To keep me sane
Of the pain
I endure, on a-daily basis
So, keep on looking,
And proceed with the whipping
You say, I desperately need.
So, when I begin to bleed,
I will just fall on my knees
And begin to pray,
For another day
To come my way.
Physically, I cannot endure this pain
But mentally, I know I will be FREE AGAIN.

ONE DAY AT A TIME

The slave in this poem describes his daily task from the time he gets up in the morning to the hottest and most stressful part of the day, it is at that time, when his master pushes him to meet certain deadlines, and although he is drained physically and mentally, he continues to live his life one day at a time.

ONE DAY AT A TIME

Before I hear the rooster's crow,
I know,
That it is time for me to rise and shine.
And go off to do a hard day's work for a man
I despise.
With the sun pounding down on my back,
I smack
The mule that pulls this groundbreaking tool.
Called a plow;
But that is how
I work faster,
But master
Say; "it aint fast enough!"
And competition is tough,
And, my level of thought has been drained
Of the pain,
Of not being able to swim across that ocean
and claim,
My true fame,
As King of my people,

A place where slaves are treated equal.
So how can I lead,
When I bleed,
With a solid-sane-mind?
I can only answer that question by taking it
ONE DAY AT A TIME.

HE CALLS US SAVAGE BEAST

Many Europeans looked at the tribal lifestyle of many African and Native American nations and labeled them as Savage Beast. The slave in this poem lets a group of his peers know that the name calling and labeling of slaves as beast, was a direct contradiction of what being Black really is. He goes on to say that; Regardless of what

Master Calls them, in the eye sights of God, they are chosen and supposed to be free.

HE CALLS US SAVAGE BEAST

He calls us savage beast
But if it wasn't for my hands
He wouldn't be able to feast
Upon the crops of this land.
He calls us savage beast,
But he does what he wants to, with my Black-Woman,
To receive pleasure and satisfaction.
And then he swears, that he is not sinning.
He calls us savage beast,
But if it wasn't for my hands digging these ditches
He wouldn't be able to enjoy the riches
I've made in this land.
He calls us savage beast,
So why couldn't he just have left me alone
In our-own homeland,
Where I, was considered; to be a FREE MAN.

MASTER'S CHILD FAVORS ME

There are many accounts of slave masters sleeping with Black Women. But this poem explains how a slave master's wife had a Mulatto child, meaning that the child was fathered by a black man. The slave thinks about telling his master the truth, but fears for the worst. All he knows is that the child favors him.

MASTER'S CHILD FAVOURS ME

Maybe if I made a run for it now, Master
won't even know.
Or maybe it's best that he found my body
frozen in the snow?
I don't know what to do?
How can I explain to master, that whenever he
goes off property,
His wife is always sending for me.
And even though Ms. Molly is the type of
woman obsessed with Black men,
Master ain't gonna believe; that whenever he's
gone,
she's always inviting me in,
To be her Slave-For-Sin.
Well this time, I guess I got off the hook,
Cause that newborn baby got all of master's
looks
And not a trait from me,
Except that curly black hair, and those big
brown eyes you see, And come to think of it,
MASTERS CHILD DO FAVOR ME.

HEY MASTER

This poem captures the thoughts of a slave as he listens to his master's directions. Picture him looking into the eyes of his master with a smile, doing everything right, but the mentality of this slave is to one day demand his freedom.

HEY MASTER

Hey master! Do you really think you can read my mind?
Because, if you could, you would never leave me behind,
The little-time I have, to plot and scheme,
Allows me time to plan my escape and think of ways to make you scream.
So, hey master! Why are you trying to drive me insane?
You have already forced me to carry your given first and last name.
But still at will
You feel you must kill,
My mental state of mind,
Which is considered; to be Devine,
But my mental capacity
Will never allow me
To develop a mentality
To stay in a state of slavery,
So, hey master! You better watch out for me.
Because the time will come, when I will demand to be FREE.

THEY SAY

Even after the Civil War, regardless of how many times America was referred to as "The Land of the Free", in most cases for Blacks, this still was not a reality. The Ex-slave in this poem has moved North after the Civil War and instead of being treated equally, he finds out that the unseen hands of slavery in the north was just as bad if not worse than the open-form in the south. He ends this poem by letting others know that only a foolish man will believe all the words of a white liar.

THEY SAY

They say that this is the land of the free!
Those are powerful words, but truthfully, it's not a reality.
They say that this is the land of the free,
Then why do these people still have me in slavery?
I thought that after the signing of the Emancipation Proclamation
I was going to get my freedom,
Because this is now a country where all men are created equal,
And even though I moved north
Of course
The hands of slavery still exist,
But they are unseen at this particular moment.
Unseen because the white man,
Has a political agenda at hand.
Unseen, because these factories that we work in,

Have the lowest pay scale for any Blackman.
When am I ever gonna wake up, from this nightmare?
When are they ever gonna accept my bronze burnt skin and wool-like hair?
God knows, because I want to do what's right,
But these people are taking my brothers lives, like thieves in the night!
Raping our women! Whenever they please!
Destroying my people on purpose and then blaming it on a disease.
Words are very powerful especially in this day,
But you will be a fool to believe everything THEY SAY.

THE LAST LAUGH OF 1863

In 1863 President Abraham Lincoln signed the Emancipation Proclamation, the document that declared all slaves in Confederate States free. Shortly after that, each slave was supposed to have been offered 40 acres and a mule. To help them get started with their new life. This poem allows you to understand that the Emancipation Proclamation was not fully enforced in all the Confederate states. For example, Texas Slaves did not get word of their freedom until 1865.

So, in actuality freedom, by that document, procrastinated the freedom of slave in certain areas, also the 40 acres and a mule was never a reality and "One Nation Under God", is just a Statement, only convenient to those in power. The slave in this poem, lets his master know that God will have the last laugh in the end.

THE LAST LAUGH OF 1863

As I sit back and reminisce of 1863
The civil war was being fought so that I maybe free
The Emancipation Proclamation,
Which was to give me my freedom throughout' this nation
Has slowly procrastinated my freedom as a man
And although I do not understand
Because now that everything seems calm and everything seems cool,
I still don't know what happened to my 40 acres and a Mule.
Well I guess you lied to me
But that's not nothing new you see,
Because how you run your government
Is why you broke, the covenant,
Of the One True Father of this nation
The Master of All Creation
The one nation under Him is what you claim to be,
But He will have the last laugh,
For all those negative things you have done to me
THE LAST LAUGH OF 1863.

FREE LABOR SLAVE

The Sorrows of Slavery

This poem explains how the birth of this country was built at the expense of many black Families. The end result shows that; most of the black workers have little or nothing to show for all the *Free Labor* their ancestors have given to this land. But they say, we free and shouldn't complain. Would you work on a job with no compensation? Many have benefited from the free labor, but we are now on an *equal playing field.*

FREE LABOR SLAVE

The day America was born,
Was the day that I was torn
Away from my family
The day my back became bloody
The day the white-man inflicted pain upon me,
Physically and mentally.
The day we sailed across the ocean for months at a time,
Chained in the bottom of a ship where millions have died.
The day America was born, was the day I never got paid,
For building this country in bondage,
AS A FREE LABOR SLAVE.

IT WON'T BE LONG

A person who cannot read is said to be uneducated and a person who is uneducated is said to be in a dead state of mind. The slave in this poem understands why teaching Blacks to read and not allowing them the right to vote was against the law. But regardless of what the white man thinks about him, he knows that GOD is the only one who can make him free.

IT WON'T BE LONG

Now I understand why I cannot read.
Because in the presence of this white-man I'll
be whipped until I bleed.
Simply because he's threatened,
From the knowledge I'm getting.
And he won't even let me vote,
Because he foolishly hopes
That others will forget about me.
Of course, he doesn't understand,
That the Most-High God has a better plan,
To resurrect this man from a dead state of
mind.
It won't be long, because master seems to be
blind,
Or he just-does not want to see,
That my father, GOD in due time will make
me FREE.

IN DUE TIME

This poem was written to explain how slaves who fought in the Civil War, kept their focus while awaiting battle. Although they still had thoughts about the wrongs of slavery, their goal was to win the Civil War. To reduce their level of stress, they would sing, dance, and pray because they knew their freedom was coming in due time.

IN DUE TIME

For many days and nights, I have longed from my freedom.
And by knowing that one day it will come
I often dance to have fun.
And even sometimes I make the mistake,
Of saying that I hate.
The one who enslaved me,
And that's not GOD-LIKE you see.
So, as I stand on the frontline
I must keep a calm mind
Because my freedom will be coming IN DUE TIME.

BLESSING FOR ME

Most slave owners saw Blacks as being inferior to whites, so they constantly overlooked the fact that slaves were very smart and clever. Not to mention "Chosen People of God"! The slave in this poem has faced a whole lot of pitfalls in his life alone, but still manages to keep a positive image of how God granting him his freedom in His time is the blessing he is waiting on.

BLESSING FOR ME

The intellectual maturity
That lies within me
Is most definitely a mystery
As it relates to the aspects of my imagination
I can only tell you about certain situations
That I've been through,
Without feeling sad, so what else can I do,
When your whole life, has been stripped and
ripped apart
Chains on our wrist and shattered dreams in
your heart,
And though my lonely spirit
Exhibits a positive image
That defines me,
As a threat to the Whiteman's society,
I will never stop telling my people of how I
once was free,
And in due time, again will be,
Because my Father God,
Has a BLESSING FOR ME.

AFRICAN DRUM

When the tools are put away and the slaves gather, they listen to the sound of a beating drum. The African-Drum was one-way slaves communicated from plantation to plantation. The message it plays could start a riot by letting them know the right time to strike or calm down by telling them when to stop. This poem explains that regardless of what the message is, music can also be used as language.

AFRICAN DRUM

I hear the sound, of the African drum, beating
in the wind, from so far away.
So, as I listen to the message it plays,
As we prance and dance around the fields,
Others run for freedom and some even plot to
kill.
The master in his sleep.
Just listen to that beat,
I don't have any money, just a whole lot of
time,
To map out my pathway to freedom that will
ease my mind.
So, continue to dance and make it look fun,
Then sprint North toward freedom, to the
sound of the AFRICAN DRUM.

THE VERY FIRST SNOW

Some slave did everything that was expected of them until certain seasons came. The slave in this poem knows the only thing separating him from freedom is a river that freezes in the winter. Regardless of how good of a job he did that benefited his master, his focus is to wait for the first large snow to come, so he can walk to freedom across the frozen water.

THE VERY FIRST SNOW

Totally not being able to understand
This man
Who say, Call him master.
As he holds the whip that strikes my back
making me work faster.
In the fields
I will.
Continue to do what I am told,
Truthfully that's only until this summer season
turns cold.
It is then I will face that cold bitter breeze of a
winter night,
When the snow is up to my knees and that
great river turns to ice.
Running off to freedom as I walk across the
frozen waters of better days,
I must pray and then say;
"Off to freedom I go, where I stop, master
won't even know.
But I will have my freedom, come THE VERY
FIRST SNOW.

FREEDOM BOUND

On the East Coast between North Carolina and Virginia there is a place called the Dismal Swamp where the dark and murky waters are filled with countless number of Underground Railroad Tails. The slave in this poem takes his chance to get freedom by getting help from many people who tells him to keep traveling north.

FREEDOM BOUND

Wadding through the dark murky waters of a swamp filled with fear.
With the sounds of the night ringing heavily in my ear.
It's hard to believe that in a couple of days.
If I keep traveling North, I will no longer be considered a slave
With the master hot on my trail,
I'll be a fool if I'm caught and returned by to the hell,
He calls home.
That's why I travel alone.
And I haven't even seen that train that runs underground,
Just a few nice folks along the way, helping me from town to town.
So, from sun-up to sun-down,
I must keep on moving because I know I'm FREEDOM BOUND.

TO GET MY FREEDOM

We hear people talk about the Underground Railroad, which was a pathway to freedom, mapped out by a series of safe houses. This poem explains how slaves who used the Underground Railroad, had to know a little bit of astronomy to pinpoint the exact directions they had to travel. Regardless of how many stars were in the sky, they knew that the North Star was the most important guide they had to get their freedom.

TO GET MY FREEDOM

As the light dances in the nighttime sky,
I don't even know why,
I must go elsewhere, to get my freedom.
So now I must use the stars to my perfection.
To pinpoint the exact direction,
I must go to get my freedom.
I guess this is the real Underground Railroad,
And that pretty, bright star, tells me that
North is the way to go.
TO GET MY FREEDOM.

THE SON HE NEVER SET FREE

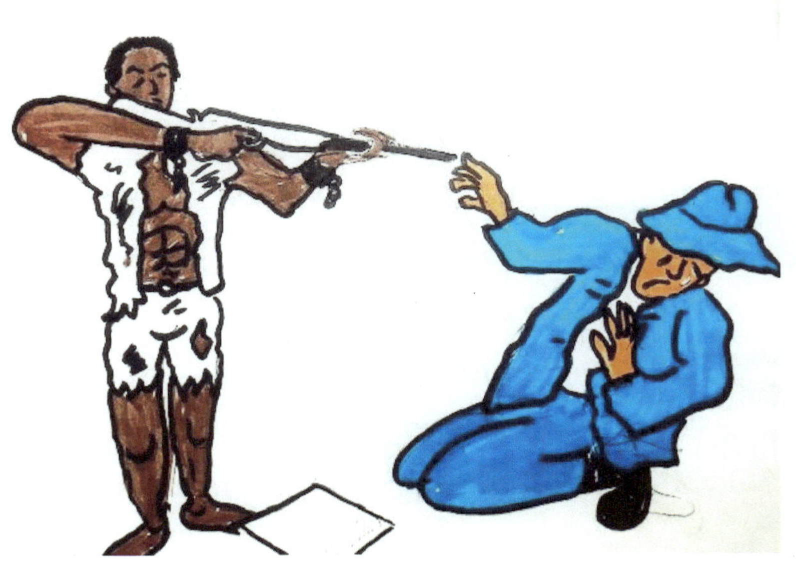

There are many accounts of how slave-owners fathered illegitimate children and did not claim them. The slave in this poem just found out the master was his daddy. So, he puts a gun to his head and asked him a few questions to see his response. In the end, he lets master live, knowing that his slave-child spared his life.

THE SON HE NEVER SET FREE

If it wasn't for my daddy,
I would probably already be free,
But as he wasted time through the years
He just forgot all about me,
The little black-white child,
That he never looked at with a smile.
The same son he created from an
inappropriate relationship
With that beautiful African Woman, he
brought from a slave-ship.
Now all of the sudden, he wants to call me his
son,
And that's only because he's on his knees
looking down the barrel of a gun,
Because if my finger wasn't on this trigger,
I guarantee he'd still call me Nigger;
That word that means ignorant,
But now that he's desperate and won't say it,
I'll just leave his life be,
So that he will always remember; THE SON
HE NEVE SET FREE.

10-LASHES OF PAIN

This poem tells a story about a slave who just received his freedom sometimes after the Civil War before leaving the plantation he decides to give his ex-master a dose of his own medicine as it relates to the beating aspects of slavery. Every lash he gives to his ex-master is justified with an explanation.

10-LASHES OF PAIN

Master! Master! Master! Now that I'm free
I'm going to give you a taste of the pain that
you forced upon me:
Get a rope, tie him up and expose that back,
And with this whip in my hand I'm going to
proceed to smack
The flesh off your back!
One!
That's for kidnapping me away from the land I
actually came FROM!
Two!
That's to let you know that this Black-Man is
whipping the skin off of YOU!
Three!
That's to make you see that you could never be
ME!
Four!
That's for raping Black women behind closed
and open DOORs!
Five!

That's for disrespecting all aspects of Black
PRIDE!
Six!
That's for all the black hearts you broke that
God has to FIX!
Seven!
That's for trying to brainwash me by not using
the Bible as a tool to get to HEAVEN!
Eight!
That's for telling slaves in Texas about their
freedom two years LATE!
Nine!
That's for confusing and destroying millions of
Black MINDS!
Ten!
That's to let you know that I will never be a
slave to you AGAIN!
And now with these ten lashes I GIVE,
Understand that this is only a fraction of what
I FEEL.

THE BUILDING OF THIS COUNTRY

The slave in this poem has lived for a long-time and regardless of the many obstacles slavery has put in the path of Blacks, he takes on the responsibility of educating people about the role black people played in developing this country.

THE BUILDING OF THIS COUNTRY

These rivers I walk beside
Sometimes freeze in the wintertime.
And these mountains that I've tried to climb,
Seem so very high at times
But I still think of better days
And other ways,
To get across this obstacle called slavery.
If my mind wasn't filled with a whole lot of
technical things,
Most of what you see,
Would probably never be.
From pyramids to trains,
I've built all sorts of things,
But they won't ever mention my name,
As the one and only creator of those things.
Even in the present history books,
They quote the notes of how they took,
Or in other words stole,
Beautifully cut diamonds and Expensive
African gold.

And let me mention the millions of lives they sold, Off into slavery,
To let everyone know I was not only a slave,
But a valued asset to THE BUILDING OF THIS COUNTRY.

I MAY BE SATISFIED

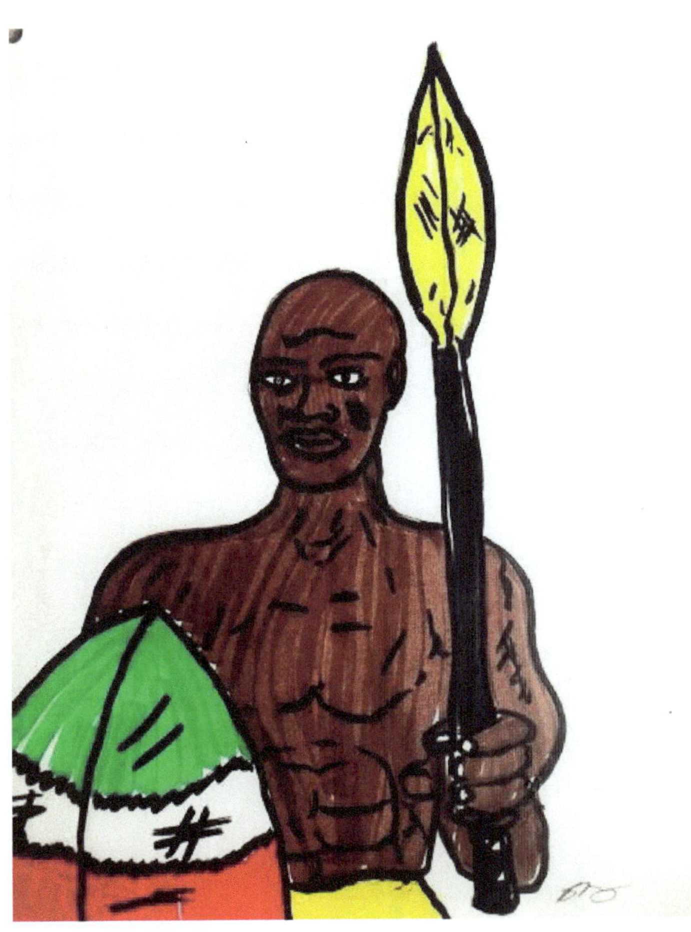

The slave in this poem pointed out a few things his ex-master could have done to ease his feelings of resentment towards him. But regardless of how bad this slave feels, he clearly points out that he is not seeking revenge on his former slave master. In the end he becomes a witness for God and tells his ex-master to repent to God for his sins, or a painful death in hell fire will be his reality.

I MAY BE SATISFIED

If you would have left me alone in the jungles of Africa,
I may be satisfied,
If you would have cut one of my limbs off and gave me my freedom,
I may be satisfied,
If you would have asked me instead of forcing me,
To help you develop your country,
I may be satisfied.
But instead
You stole the knowledge and wisdom out of my head,
And for now, you must face the facts of reality
That after this Civil War when I will become free,
Someone is going to pay you back for the negative things,
You have done to me,
And weather its physically,

Or mentally,
It really doesn't matter,
But don't just fear me;
Watch out for that cook that makes your biscuit batter,
So, in other words think twice,
About that slave woman that seems so nice,
And when she hands you that cool refreshing drink
With crushed glass mixed with ice,
You will begin to die a slow death,
And when you take your last breath,
No! I won't be glad because your life is about to end,
But I will be satisfied when you ask God to forgive your sins,
And that's when I will be SATISFIED.

THE TRUE 4TH OF JULY

This poem describes the reality of how some slaves fought for the freedom of this country during the American Revolution. The slave in this poem decides to stick by his master instead of running to Canada for Great Britain who guaranteed slaves their freedom. In the end after fighting for the *land of the free*, the slave was still in chains and the reality of freedom was only for the white-man.

THE TRUE 4TH OF July

I fought for this county on the 4th of July,
I fought for this county and never understood why;
While I was staring at the stars and stripes of glory,
Thinking my freedom was guaranteed so I didn't have to worry.
"Freedom for All!" was shouted from the British side,
And while some slave ran quickly to those words, I stood and fought with pride,
Fighting with all my heart, because I knew I would be free,
But after the smoke had cleared and the war was won, those chains were still on ME.

LAST AND EVIL DAYS

The slave in this poem is a deeply religious man, who prophesied to his slave-master that his life will end soon, and he needs to repent for the evil act of slavery.

LAST AND EVIL DAYS

When the walls of this world come tumbling down,
Where will you be, when God comes around?
Master you just don't want to admit, your days have been numbered
Because, if I could take over your Reign of Terror.
My enslaved Blackface will always be the vision you'll remember.
The marks on my back the salt in my wounds,
Your half-bread children from a Black-Woman's womb.
You have a whole lot of repenting to do,
But don't let these few words I say, frighten the life out of you.
But before I go,
I just have to let you know,
Regardless of what you say,
On this here day,
If you don't repent for your sins,

Eternity you will burn, from the outside in.
So repent and be saved, repent and be save,
So that God can have mercy on your life in
these LAST AND EVIL DAYS.

FREEDOM CHEERS

During the middle and late and 1700's the Island of Hatti was desired by many European nations because of its lucrative sugar cane industry. A black carriage driver named Toussaint Louverture saw that the number of Blacks on the island outnumber the whites. So, he organized and became the General of the Haitian Revolution that put an end to the white man's rule in Haiti. The message of this successful revolt got back to America, which gave those slaves hope of winning their own freedom that somewhat came in 1863 which was 72 years after 1791.

FREEDOM CHEERS

In 1791 about half a million blacks
Were in fact
The driving force behind the sugarcane industry
On that island we call Haiti.
And being fed up with the white-man's rules,
Turned my human nature from kind to cruel,
That's why my Country is in the midst, of a revolution.
Because I have solved the simple solution
Of knowing who was, the true enemy,
Walking on the grounds of my property.
I was the carriage driver in disguise,
Although I smiled, my true feelings for that man lies deep within my eyes,
So, I organized a revolt
That choked the hopes
Of a white man's rule forever,
Sending a message straight to America.
So, in 72 years, those slaves too can sing their own FREEDOM CHEERS.

EARLY IN THE MORNING

With the numerous amounts of runaway slave stories passed down from generation to generation, this poem explains how two slaves made a run for their freedom. As they comfort each other and rest, they realize that they only have a few more hours until morning and then they will be free.

EARLY IN THE MORNING

On the run, with my beautiful Black Queen,
It seems,
That this day will never end.
So, we tend to rest,
The best,
Way we can,
By staying out of sight, from the white man.
You know the one who enslaved us from the start,
The one who put scars on our bodies and shattered dreams in our hearts,
The one who sold my father and mother,
The one who raped my sister and tortured my brother!
But for now, I'll just rest
On the Breast
Of my beautiful Back-woman
And think of how freedom will come, EARLY IN THE MORNING.

WHITE FRIENDS AND FAMILY

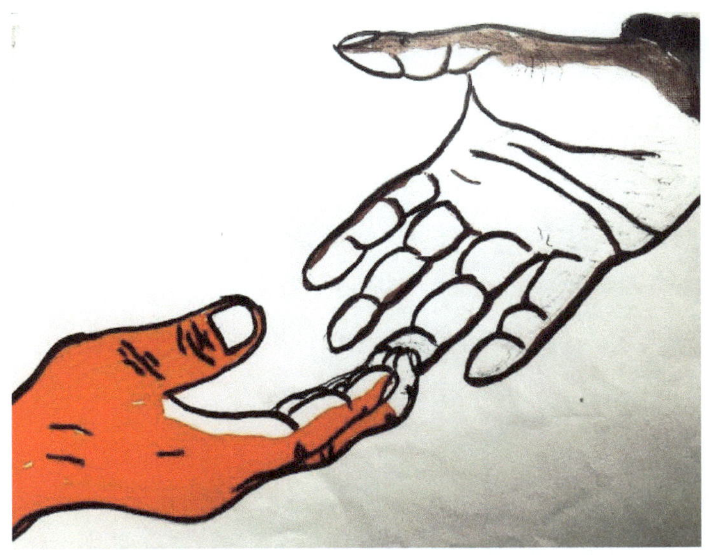

This poem explains how some white people who did not agree with the institution of slavery risked their own lives and helped runaway slaves travel North to get their freedom. The slave in this poem has been taken in by a white family who hides him in the basement of their home, and when the slave-catchers appear, the family tells them they are home alone and have not seen any run-aways. Some whites looked at slavery as a curse that followed God's chosen people, so they felt obligated to help them. Others knew that slavery was wrong, and they had to help at any cost.

WHITE FRIENDS AND FAMILY

Not all white people like to see me in chains,
And some even claim to feel my pain,
As they help me board that train,
that travels north to freedom
You didn't even see them,
Hide me in the basement of their homes,
And then told those slavecatchers
They been home, for most of the Day
I'll say,
Not all white people, agree with the institution of slavery,
And some even risked their lives for me to be free,
So, I can truly say; that some white people to me are most definitely
MY FRIENDS AND FAMILY.

BROKEN DOWN RESERVATION

When the first Europeans arrived in America, they introduced themselves as friends. Many of the natives welcomed the white man and shared their land and ideas with them. Present history books state that Native Americans taught settlers a variety of skills essential for survival. Even with that the Europeans became full of greed and focusing on their own selfish needs. In the end many native tribes were cheated out of and kicked-off of their land and placed on reservations.

BROKEN DOWN RESERVATION

When I first met the white man
I welcomed him with open arms
And also taught most of them how to farm
And then saved them from a very harsh
winter,
By sharing and preparing a nice thanksgiving
dinner,
And even after all of that,
He still proceeded to stab me in the back,
By stealing my land with evil persuasions,
Then putting me and my people,
On BROKEN DOWN RESERVATION.

IF I WAS FREE

The slave in this poem is just thinking how freedom would feel for him. No chains or demands and he will be able to enjoy the benefits of the land, not being whipped or having the fear of his family being sold to another plantation or having to share his wife. In other words, if he was free, he would have a better opportunity.

IF I WAS FREE

If I was free, like I ought to be,
This so, called white master, wouldn't have
these chains on me.
If I was free like I ought to be,
I could work these lands and reap the benefits
for me and my family.
If I was free like I ought to be,
When I get tired, I can relax in the shade, and
not worry about master whipped me,
If I was free, liked I ought to be,
No one would ever be given the opportunity,
to do these things to me.

YOUR LAST BREATH

Many times, to install fear in the mind of slaves, the slave-master would make examples out of runaways by chopping off a foot, whipping, hanging, or burning them on a tree. The slave in this poem has just been hung from a tree and set on fire. Before he dies, he asks his killers; to think about who they will have to answer to before their last breath.

YOUR LAST BREATH

It seems that this day will never end,
With a rope around my neck and fire set to my skin.
This has only happened because I wanted to be free,
And some of those evil doers feel that I shouldn't be.
When can we be truly looked at as equal people?
In this so-called Land of the Free, I am burned dead or alive,
And you have the audacity to question; "Why I believe in Black Pride."
Close your eyes and picture the death and destruction my people have seen.
Or are you scared to face the reality of having a repeated bad dream?
Babies cut out of mothers and crushed with bare feet,
Families ripped apart as the black child weeps.

Placed with the animals in a barn filled with hay.
Traumatized and beaten, when we don't do what master say.
As I hang high and die as you celebrate my death,
Think about who you will answer to when you take YOUR LAST BREATH.

BEFORE SUNRISE

When some slaves ran for their freedom in the rain, they often had to seek shelter anywhere they could. The salve in this poem has found a place to escape the stormy weather, while he makes himself comfortable, he is confident that his master's dogs lost his trail in the rain, giving him the opportunity to think about his past and his future of being free, before sunrise.

BEFORE SUNRISE

As the rain begins to pour down,
I hear the sound
Of it
Dropping on the shed
Where I lay my head.
On the hay-made-mattress and potato sack spreads.
Do you really what to know, all the trouble I have been through?
From being enslaved in a cage like an animal in the zoo.
The sands of my land, is constantly being stained
By the pollutants and things of the Whiteman's brain.
Now I run
Not for fun.
But from the scent of those dogs
And the flesh-piercing bullets of master's gun.
I guess he lost my trail in the rain this time,
And there won't be a next time,
Because, I will have my-freedom BEFORE THE SUNRISE.

FREEDOM I TRULY ADORE

The slave in this poem is reminiscing about the day he lost his freedom. At first, he was running freely in his county and then he was taken away in chains and know freedom is only a thought he longs for.

FREEDOM I TRULY ADORE

Freedom! Freedom! Freedom! Is the only thing
I think about,
Because there use to be a time,
When I could run
And have fun
In the sun
But all of that has been taken away from me
Simply because I ran freely in my county.
One moment I was playing,
And the next, I was saying:
"Let me go! Please!"
Then I dropped to my knees
And proceeded to pray,
But when I opened my eyes, that bad dream
still didn't go away.
So, as I drag these heavy chains across the
ground and on the floor,
All I can think about is freedom, that feeling I
have no more,
Freedom, that feeling, I TRUELY ADORE.

HARRIET TUBMAN

Whenever the Underground Railroad is mentioned, the name Harriet Tubman is always brought up. Harriet Tubman was an abolitionist leader who made about 19 trips back to the south and free an estimated 300 slaves. One of her nicknames was Black Moses. This poem explains how she never used her gun but made it plain and clear to slaves who traveled with her that she would shoot them dead, if they decided to turn back.

HARRIET TUBMAN

About 19 times her journey was made,
Back to the south to free an estimated 300
slaves.
Stay on Track and follow that star North,
And in due time we will be free,
But if you decided to turn back,
A bullet to the back
Is the only Master you'll see.
And although she never killed
Because that wasn't Gods will
She still, kept a gun by her side,
And for every journey made,
Before she transported slaves
She had to look in their eyes,
"if you want to be free,
Then you need to come with me"
Is the phrase she often said,
Risking her life,
And never thinking twice,
About the slavecatchers who wanted her dead.

Leading slaves to freedom,
So, their Master could not mistreat them.
Ignoring the price on her head.
We call her Black Moses,
That strong black woman,
HARRIET TUBMAN, HARRIET TUBMAN.

BLACK KINGS AND QUEENS

The slave in this poem is free and he reflects on the current state of the Kings and Queens who were brought to this land and stripped of their heritage. Although they are currently free, they are still sleep mentally.

BLACK KINGS AND QUEENS

Whoever thought that I was a King?
And she was a Queen?
My ancestors were bought here on ships in chains,
Stripped of their heritage and given the Slave Masters names.
So, I could not have been a king and she could not have been a queen?
Do you really understand what I mean?
Separated by complexions,
And sent away in different directions,
Suppressed by my current reality,
But God is showing favor in this changing society,
Royalty leeks from my blood, sweat and tears,
The truth of who I am will finally be revealed,
But only to the few that are awoke and chosen,
Because many of the kings and queens are asleep and frozen

In the system that allows them to stay sleep in a dream
And denounce their true heritage as
BLACKKINGS AND QUEENS.

BLACK WOMAN

BLACK WOMAN

Black Woman, the flawless pearl of Perfection,
Black Woman, your presence makes the wind change Directions.

And whether, you are light, medium or dark skinned in Complexion,
You have always been there, through thick and thin Situations.

From the beginning of Time,
You have installed within my Mind.
The perfect vision of a Woman,
People should bow down when they see you Coming,
Because you are the Queen of every continents Coastline,
Most men from your own homeland and different Nations,
Should put you on a pedestal

And thank you for giving birth to all
Civilizations,
But the ones who know this, but choose not to
Understand,
To me you are still the Perfect Jewel,
BLACKWOMAN, BLACKWOMAN
UNDERSTAND!

STRONG WOMAN

Strong Woman, the flawless pearl of
Perfection,
Strong Woman, your presence makes the wind
change Directions.

And whether, you're light, medium or dark
skinned in Complexion,
You have always been there, through thick and
thin Situations.

From the beginning of Time,
You have installed within my Mind.

The perfect vision of a Woman,
People should bow down when they see you
Coming,

Because you are the Queen of every continents
Coastline,
Most men from your own homeland and
different Nations,

Should put you on a pedestal
And thank you for giving birth to all
Civilizations,

But the ones who know this, but choose not to
Understand,
To me you are still the Perfect Jewel,
STRONG WOMAN, STRONG WOMAN
UNDERSTAND!

ABOUT THE AUTHOR

Benjamin Franklin Burum, Jr currently resides in Houston Texas with his Wife Sheila Burum and he is the proud father of 5 children: 4 boys and 1 girl. Benjamin is an Educator, Advocate, Writer, Mentor and Pastor of Faith Seeds of God Crusade Ministries, Inc. He was born in a small town on the East Coast of North Carolina called; Edenton. As a young child, he was a very artist, winning countless number of art contest and competed in local and statewide talent shows from Elementary to High School. After receiving his Diploma from John A. Holmes High School. He attended Johnson C. Smith University in Charlotte North Carolina where he ran track, participated in a variety of community activities, and received a Bachelor of Arts degree in History. And he holds a Master of Arts Degree in Teaching from Kaplan University.

In 1996 after visiting the Black Holocaust Museum in Houston TX, he would write parts of poems that seemed insignificant. But as he found himself performing and using his work to educated students, it became evident that his work clearly captured the thoughts and feelings of slaves while they were in captivity. Out of that thought, "The Sorrows of Slavery: Poetry of the Past" was created. Completed in 1996 and copywritten in 1998. After a few years of performing throughout the Houston poetry scene he began to only promote his poem; Black Woman/Strong Woman and a few other pieces as he advocated for young men locally and assisted orphaned children Uganda Africa.

As he continued to balance his commitment to Education and the Community by Mentoring young Men, he organized the poems in a white binder and only recited some of the poetry during Black History Month, while this master piece just collected dust on a shelf.

During the Summer of 2018, while sitting with family and friends going thru photos and art work, Benjamin was asked by his Brother-n-Law who is the founder of Greatness University from the United Kingdom Professor Dr. Patrick Businge; "Why was this not published in book format?" With no excuse to give; Benjamin was asked to organize the book so that it could be published. And know that it is finished, a fire has been rekindled. *"The Steps of a Good Man is ordered by the Lord: and he delighteth in his way," Psalm 37:23.*

www.ingramcontent.com/pod-product-compliance
Lightning Source LLC
Chambersburg PA
CBHW041407010726
47507CB00001B/32

* 9 7 8 1 9 1 3 1 6 4 4 0 9 *